SAFE GROUND

Rosie Johnston

Safe Ground
published in the United Kingdom in 2025
by Mica Press & Campanula Books

https://micapress.uk | contact@micapress.uk

ISBN 978-1-869848-40-8

Truth is the only safe ground to stand on.

Elizabeth Cady Stanton

Contents

Carnlough Bay
Cleopatra on Portstewart Strand
Palm Tree Victory
In Good Hands
A World Away
She's Staying
Abercorn, 4 March, 1972: Six O'clock
Glitterball
My Boyish Love
Reflection
C Sharp
Six-Count Jive Extracts
On a Scale of One to Ten
Bloodstains on the Stones
Breathe in the View
Safe Ground
Off the Map
Being with Anne
Seasalter
High Winds
Away in a Beach Hut
In the Cool of This Hottest Day
Oyster Seventeens
Pure Blue
Happy the Woman
Just the Ticket
Nayland Rock Shelter, 2022
Laughing and Grief: Paris, 2020

Acknowledgements

Carnlough Bay

Earth is tawny
corduroy tonight, and burnt
blood clods. Charolais cows, peach
white going on amber, slant their paintbrush lashes
at the limestone cliffs.

Sunset's gold-spill gets me every time.
Come on, I'll take your hand, let's run like oystercatchers
along the line between water and earth, make the
biggest splashes in the tiniest waves, relish
edges between land and
sea and us and air.
Here, where
no people
are,
I breathe. Expand again, at last, to my full size. I'm
tallest in bare feet, on sea-rolled shingle, back
heavy in my heels, cupping the weight of
whelk shells in my pockets.
Constant in it all, so
many years, the
need for
sea.

Cleopatra on Portstewart Strand

The barge she sat in, like a burnish'd throne,
Burned on the water: the poop was beaten gold;
Purple the sails, and so perfumed that
The winds were lovesick with them…
Shakespeare's 'Antony and Cleopatra', Act II, sc. 2:

There she was, all happy helplessness,
that purple car of hers, sun-glossed
in its evening wear,
chrome hubcaps silvered by the waves,
us wee'uns in matching goosepimples
home-knit jumpers yelling to go home,
even if it did mean ten green bottles yet again.

Intoxicated by the first whiff of beach air,
she would never park where we were told,
always drove the chariot straight to the palest sand.
Yanked the brake on hard, raced all giggles and squeals
to lose her usual scent of chip fat and onions in the surf
before she draped herself in a deckchair
strapless, guiltless, matchless in her
heedlessness of anyone.

That day no gravity applied,
not even when, past home time,
the day's shine deep in her laugh lines,
the car refused to leave.

More throttle dug us deep,
ignored all blandishment and blarney.
'Everybody out'; she honked and clamoured:
'Heave!' We wee'uns shoved alright,
shoulders to the car. Slowly
smiling fathers came to help.
Exhaust fumes swathed us all,
sand and seaweed flying,
lipstick on her teeth, the long red nails

urging from the window,
'Come on, come on!'
and high above the racket
seagulls cackled
and all the men
adored her.

PALM TREE VICTORY

For Auntie Jean and her school house in County Down

The doll knew - her eyes swung shut as I laid her flat on my pyjamas
beside the toothbrush. Closed the lid.
'We're going to the palm tree,'
I whispered.

Those little catches on the suitcase, I still feel victory
in my thumbs, the way I jiggled that lid,
nursed the metallic welcome,
pressed hard
shut.

I felt the doll's smile as we drove, the lot of us,
through the Dark Hedges,
round the Cave Hill, south
through Saintfield and Crossgar,
to the lee of the Mournes,

in drizzle. All the way, suitcase on my lap,
doll smiling, silent.

Beside our car, sunshine slants its goodbyes from Donard's peak.
'We're away now,' goes my mother.
'I've got my things,' I say,
always the good wee girl.
The suitcase swings arm's length.

'I'm staying here,' I say, loud. 'For ever.'

Mayhem.
One brother weeps in the car, hiding.
The other - opportunist - takes flying kicks at my shins.

I stand my ground. Ignore them, me and the doll smiling.

My mother: 'In the car, now!'

Cracks her knuckles.
My father's lower tones with Jean.

The palm tree catches a southerly off
Commedagh, loosens one long
sword-leaf, khaki, curled at the hilt,
twirls it in a flicker-pirouette to tarmac at my feet.

Jean smiles: 'That settles it.' My father
laughs, 'This once, just once she stays.'

I turn, stride into
Auntie Jean's house and mount her green stairs.

Thumbs pulsing.

In Good Hands

Little Seven, your sentry look - that
level
stare's already ancient.

His whiskey glows by your bedside lamp,
'Read Trojan Horse
again, Daddy.'

Aeneas's tears at the mural of sorrows,
Achilles'
battle rage: he plays them all.

He weaves a lifelong wonderland:
Priam, Mozart,
the Clancys, Keats.

On the kitchen stool you turn - turn - turn -
she hems
your skirt, sly-pins your thigh.

This time your soundless tears won't
blink away.
She smacks your calf: 'Shut up, you.'

She's a stove you look after
day and night
or her tolerance blows out.

Both eyes drip, her come-with-me fist
grips
your arm: 'When I leave him, you're mine.'

Downstairs something crashes.
Are they
dancing tonight? Another skirmish?

You grow nimble on those seismic plates,
the dancefloor
of their masquerade.

Mother is high on the see-saw
again.
When will she really see you?

Upturn that doll's cot - its painted base is
your desk:
your best oasis.

Between parents' shouts and brothers' clouts,
you steer
that lifeline desk unbowed.

Little Seven, you will be safe -
I will
    never leave go your wee hand.

A World Away

In the close of a nightmare's eye,
I'm seven again,
back from school alone.

A walk of a mile down the road to the big shops,
dash across it to where she left me once, her heart
so high with dresses and hats, she forgot
I might need help up into the bus behind her.

'The long face on the wee'un,'
she laughed later.
'Tears trippin' it.'
I don't remember tears. I do still
see the twisted shout-face on her
yet again I botched her life
and me left on the pavement
still shiny wet in my memory.

Other days we were a foursome,
or a threesome and me:
my brothers huddled emperor toddlers
under the pram hood
in her triangle of intimacy.
The pram handle was mine,
its stream of chrome reflections
a world away from her voice.

The house is closed. Locked up.
I'm round the back, sopping in drizzle.
I need to pee. Overcome and standing there,
I feel it hot
down into my shoes.
On no, the shoes.
Bruises will scud through her anger,
join the storm clouds already on my legs,
I cry, I cry
for the smacks to come

The swing of the side gate, no coat, no time,
her raw vowels never so welcome, here's
Ruby and I'm up in her arms, the red felt hat
pinned to her perm, squeezed cig in flow:
'I'm baking curny scones,' she says,
'come on and help me.'
Her kitchen fug swirls around me.
Off come the guilty shoes. Persian cats
pick through flour scattered wide across her table.
One sits on my feet.
Hot milk by the Raeburn.
Ruby's laughter billows, childless Ruby, my other mother,
who other-mothers all us quiet ones, she talks. We talk.
We sing together: '*My aunt Jane, she called me in.*'

When my shoes are dry enough,
we tuck blackberry plants into their garden beds.
My job is to wrap muck around their feet
to keep them warm until the spring,
minding for thorns while the big russet leaves
lick and tickle my hands.
Planted in October rain, Ruby says,
they'll root throughout the hail and snow.
Next year's berries juicier for their hard start.
Hunkered together, we hear the car in the road.
Ruby's stubby fingers rush to brush
my palms clean
in sunlight.

She's Staying

She tried to leave again last night, skirl of tyres, the car's roar
heard from our beds, away to the beach. We found her crying,
north wind in her face, over limpets in a rippled pool.

But today we've a houseful of neighbours.
Guests swap their patter, mutter, worry about the Derry news
but Uncle Jim's OK this time, that's something.

A wail above it all - my mother's curled on the carpet
round the whiskey bottle, new black dress rucked up. 'Your father's
gone', she wails, she wants to die, 'where is he, Rosie, find him'

Gales screech off Donegal, tangle my hair over my face.
My teacher's car, lamplit outside our house, spindrift on the roof,
two heads inside, in silhouette against the moon-gleam road.

Sleet cuts the breath from me. I judder. Coward, I go back inside.
Mother yells more bluster in my face. It's somehow all my fault. I am
a razor clam shut tight. Up the stairs two at a time.

The crowd still throbs downstairs. She's laughing now,
'We'll have a wee dance, you and me, c'mon now, sing with me:
There may be troubles ahead…'

Dad's guitar, his easy baritone above the chatter,
Star of the County Down, for the love of his life,
his wife, his one and only her.

I sit on my bed. The floor trembles to cheers, applause below.

The last of the singers is fading down the road. My parents,
their voices knit
in wary tenderness, pad to their room. The door ticks shut.

She's staying.

Abercorn, 4 March, 1972: Six O'Clock

Our local news: usually a brew of hoax bombs,
near misses, 'legitimate targets', platitudes.
This time the young reporter from the scene
is still in his coat: mostly women
in the café, he said, wee girls after school
maimed - he stopped, sucked air in hard
Two dead. Bomb under a table. In a hold-all
His shoulders shuddered high, the coat big on him now.
'Hold-all.'
Eyes unfocussed, he managed the when and where of it:
Castle Lane. Bill O'Hara's place. Across from McManus's where we
went for school shoes. Belfast's dead centre. Then
he cried.   Stumbled away off the screen.

Colleagues rounded things off, gave numbers for enquiries.
In the bar later they'd learn him how the cold steel of drink
carves sobs out of your heart, cauterises wounds in the soul
before you've even felt them, trundles you through the dirty years.

Over his shoulder we'd all seen it: the beast was out of its cage.
Chill control, red-eyed in our homes, ready to clot our lives.
The lowest we can be was loose. Nothing mattered now but blood.

Most had no choice but to stay - even when they'd
lost all - to hirple on, patch up, work for peace
in the throat of that stinking scorch-breath.
Families urged us youngsters to safety, to learn
wherever we went,
humanity's brute underside's no household pet.
It sleeps, slavers, rears up, yanks a leash
and we stumble, dazed by gore.
Every time it swings its horns,
another tenable treaty is torn,
another flimsy hope of rescue
from its monstrous rule is gone.

Glitterball

Portnahapple's rock pool after school.
A northerly stirs goosebumps on my thighs.
Granite stipples pinch my naked soles.
In far-off downpours ocean vessels, mink-
soft to my bookish eyes, breathe love sighs
to this land-locked girl. I stretch, rise, dive -

At home, a stroll away, a letter bids,
come. Study. Learn new people. City life.
Swap arctic terns for lectures and Sauterne,
spurn seaweed tickles in raw surf for stern
discernment, call it 'taste', you'll never yearn
for icy swims or wheeling gulls again.

I skip between the cracks on shiny streets.
I work, commute, drink, speak as London does,
the accent on the money, on panache.
Watch my children grow to navigate this
mishmash glitterball that bounces all our
sparks into one lustrous galaxy. Yet -

in every tube-train's creak, a seagull laughs.
With every passing van, a swish of surf.

My Boyish Love

(response to Shakespeare's sonnet 126 for Live Canon's 154 Project, 2016)

My boyish love. Your solemn
tacit beauty
enchanted even time

till in this willowed place you
chose to wane
in earth, while my heart waxes.

Your stone preserves your name,
once mine.
Chiselled dates deny vitality.

We linked hands and birled in
nature's blessings,
snubbed her warnings, let them swirl.

Love led us from discredit to
debit. Time
divided us in two.

I survived the severed decades
to unite here
stricken at your grave.

My heart still whirls with
precious, youthful
you.

Reflection

Mirror, you old jobsworth, you know
all my fractures and keep your counsel.

Half-turn. There - twelve years old,
my scowl, half confidence, half hope of better.

Eyes dip, and I'm in an aisle. A dress
my mother liked and I did not.

Veiled dreams. That need to please,
appease, make good, make safe.
Make it out of there.

Between my brows one line of anguish
cut two years later when he left.

Sly memory: it skims the worst
away as if it never happened.

Decades splinter into gemstone shards
we sift, remix with artful ease.

You, mirror, witness all our pieces,
sparkle-dust of loss and kisses.

C Sharp

In Golding's Lord of the Flies, Jack expects to be the boys' chief, as he's head boy and chapter chorister, and because he can sing 'C sharp'.

Where do you hide your cruel streak?
In the soft roll of your lapel,
your Gatsby cuffs, that Zinfandel,
or in your practised stream of jokes,
mock deference your masterstroke?

In your aubergine silk lining,
with tears your mother shed beside
your cot, her taut face belying
terror that you could be dying…
(so you said - or were you lying?)

Below the tongues of hand-made boots
you'd rarely stoop to shine yourself?
Stowed with your brother's school reports
in Art and Latin, French and graphs
where he came first, and you fell short?

In the pocket of your chinos
ironed by your Filipina,
with the handkerchief you tightened
round your playground fist, eyes bright and
stark, to prove you were not frightened?

In Grandpapa's black velvet coat
between his wild-oats anecdotes
and countless grand-paternal gloats?
Does your father's best-loved corkscrew
bequeath it, twist by twist, to you?

Behind your tiepin, do you keep
the sundry times that girls said no
but got it anyway and you
blamed them for weeping in your sleep
and laughed at them and called them cheap?

Or – bundled underneath your bed
as far as little hands could shove,
surrounded by the nights you prayed
for rescue from a prelate's love:
your surplice, age ten, cut to shreds?

Did printed sheets of choral song
compact the hours you used to long
to crash through doorways, run headlong
and punch and bleed till nobody
dared mention God or family?

However great your wealth or power,
the need stays with you every hour:
find pleasures somehow that won't sour,

outrace that bare-faced, base embrace,
erase debasement's every trace.
Know peace in loving's tender grace.

Extracts from *Six-Count Jive*

Lie soft, gentle winged creature, roped and dazed;
you're safe
unless you struggle.

V
'Define me by my best,' he whimpers,
foulness
stowed beneath his cassock.

Fear arches her, venom-fangs rise
blood-hot
to rip the threat to slivers.

Consummatum est. It's done.
The truth's
been said: new prayers will be heard.

IX
Up she flowed - a dove high above
danger -
watched her own body slumped, splayed.

The body flinched. Jolted. Fell
back on the floor.
She observed it whimper.

Foxes scuffle, wail. In pitch-black
hush,
her body's alarms scream riot.

Dawns a walking, shoreline truth:
tormentors
debase no-one but themselves.

On a Scale of One to Ten

The questionnaire slips to the floor.
A gust from the window spins it and years ago my son's boat
drifts on the town pond more and more out of reach.
A tear rolls down my cheek. Is this me now,
where questions pared of all sensitivity
rate me formally beyond normality
on a scale of one to ten?

My inner song replies,
'Just go, those questions aren't for you,
you're coming through.

You've had a bad case of bad, bad husband
but you're not sinking. Life shines in you,
clinks round and light in your fingers, new minted.
Savour it with fresh-baked rolls mallow soft, floured,
plump. Feel it slobber you like a month-old puppy
climbing up your sleeves to suck your ears.
Be bold. Let new days laugh away old fears.
You're smiling, look, first time in years
air rushes into you deep. Don't
think, don't waste this precious,
brief today, don't even pray,
just let your hands
fall open.'

Bloodstains on the Stones

Wolf-memories weave around my legs.
Docile now.
I tiptoe. Whisper.

Wolf-memories startle. Leap up, snap,
shove me over,
rip at my throat.

Wolf-memories lap my blood, slump
against my ribcage,
snarl in their sleep.

Wolf-memories wake when they like.
Leave
when they like. When they have done with me.

Wolf-memories rise, shake free, lick
themselves clean.
Saunter outside. Sated.

Sunlight through curtains. I
finger-search
for wounds. Test my feet beneath me.

Each fray with the wolves leaves me
stronger,
they say. More restored.   I hate wolves.

Breathe in the View

Here in my sanctuary, between these apple saplings
where sea gales wash my heart,
I pull up my past by the thickest stems.
A tough pull, both arms. My back into it.

Roots reach spectre-white in the dusk.
I shake the whole palaver, curse, brush
thorns and thread-spines off my hands, then
sling it.
I stretch, breathe in the view, and sing.

Not today the old songs of men in crested helmets
where rivals' gore combines in distant rivers,
their blood unites in sterile mud,
yet somehow that is victory.

I sing of the home wars: blood pooled in toilet bowls,
humiliations stacked, cracked dishes in the sink,
bruises never seen, silent childhoods swung lifeless, gone
faster than a fairground ride

Let's waltz though to the rhythms of hospital wards,
boogie to the fugues of family,
salsa to the pulse of beloved kitchens,
chant shanties to the valour of escape.

Sing with me of forgiveness.
Throughout my winter dark its call
grated like a deathbed rasp. Yet here
in a young gull's wingbeat whistle,
rich as twenty blooms on a forgotten tree,
its aria steeps this splintered heart.

Safe Ground

I

Gravid time. Still air. A drop
hanging
from a leaf. A wish unspoken.

Happed up birthling, you're
all trust
in my arms, ready for home. Into sleet.

I hold the clock's hands, wrest
this hour to a stop
while you sleep in my lap.

In each lark's heartbeat, each spider's
stitch, each
baby-blink, love stretches, yawns.

A gleam. Breath held I watch
my baby
reach - two steps, one step, three - and walk.

II

Your teens thunder through me,
blades on your wheels
harrowing your world and mine.

'This King and Queen no good,' you wail.
'Deal me
another set of parents.'

Minefield child, I never knew when
my tread
or yours could slaughter us both.

In one foul choppy squall
our boat stalled.
We foundered in that crash-dive sea.

You beckon from your father's
quicksand,
step closer, half smile – and are gone.

Around me again spins the sky's wheel
rising in hope,
setting in loss.

You are loved, sweet child,
wherever you are,
whatever you dare become.

III

'What are you weaving, Grandma?'
Wool glides
between the old woman's knuckles.

'Just sorrow, dearest' - Grandma
tightens a thread -
'the weft of our lives.'

IV

My daily whispered love swoops
on the wind:
never would I cast you loose.

A tear dangles from long
telepathic wires
and at last you phone me.

Still my hand's refused. Pocketed.
The hand
that fed you in your highchair.

Both bereft, our lungs cough up, with ancient
foetid air,
bright clots of truth.

Between 'I love you' and 'the real me'
stretch
layers of wary détente.

For there it is, inheritance,
not just in
eyes or chin: in backbone.

Beside a silver-quill sunset
simplicity
walks us to safe ground.

Pride: a stunted, one-eyed word for
lungfuls
of relief my child's so strong.

Our eyes see our children grown.
Our hearts
still cradle our swaddled newborns.

Off the Map

For RR Johnston who pioneered the F-M rock climb on Slieve Lamagan, County Down in 1949

'Descent's the toughest part, hard on the knees.'
He rubs his barrel-knotted fingers
over boulders of arthritis in his own.
It's his younger self talking, the lad in his twenties
who zigzagged Mournes crags and cliffs, unnamed
until he and his friends, no satnav, no phones, claimed
the likes of the Raven's Nest and 'the F-M'.

Silence.
He's away, remembering. That chuckle in his eyes,
the one that hooked the women.
Here comes the story:
in towering rain, well off the map, their army surplus sodden,
his cheap wee gutties useless on that mossy
upper slab so off they came, shoved
dizzy dazed into his jacket,
sock soles,
no going back though upward felt like
overhang, pure balance,
the mountain itself
tipping him back
into air

'til there it was,
the edge - rough to the finger whorls but
it's a hold. A teetering clamber up against the winds,
downpour still sheeting his glasses,
he twisted into place and sat.
Fuck me, he breathed.

Alive. Fuck me! Loud, lusty, and his friend laughed too,
full-chested cheers away beyond the fields below
their bellowed primal whoop at sheer survival.
So, that's what that ascent became: '*The F-M.*'

Fuck me. My father's life could have skidded,
bounded, slithered down the rocks,
crashed in gorse and heather,
quenched in some sheuch,
trickle-bled away
before my spark lit.

My own ascents are unnamed.
Back from an awkward descent,
one lonely step, another, skidding, losing grip
in howling gusts, my oldest agonies reclaiming me
then weary-wake all night, I know nothing but that I too
have been somewhere
exceptional.

On my knee, my father's compass. Its metal finger
tinkles against the glass case, swings like a dancer
around the neat, blue capital letters of the winds.
This tiny wheel measured distance on his maps,
proper maps in the browns, greens, ochres,
dirty snow-greys of the land itself.
At the top this round link here is
to wear it, as I do, so you're
close to me, Dad.

Still my belay.

Being with Anne

In scarves and our hoods up, bare toes in the rough sand,
crunched mussels and scraps of mermaids' purses,
we sing to the full moon in Newcastle.

Squalls laden with drizzle prowl the horizon,
howl across the hackles of the waves,
force our eyes half closed, rip sound from our mouths

but we belt out the old song anyway
where our beloved Mournes
sweep down to the sea.

For all of my travels, to London and all,
I'm home, heart half-empty but for the treasure
Auntie Anne gave me years ago:

At Granny's I'm out of the way while a brother is born.
We chase hens, feed mucky pigs, birl in the garden,
link daisy chains, shine buttercups under our chins.

At pyjama time, Anne folds around me to read a wee story.
We fall laughing at her Granny-wolf teeth as big as pig's tusks.
'Again, Anne, please again!' And she did, she always did.

Every time, in Red Riding Hood's forest, the pair of us
whispered jokes and bird songs to the darkness
and Anne wove trust into our togetherness.

Her sofa blanket is pure wool, no pretence about Anne,
in her favourite colours: hen-feather tawny, sunset bronze,
saffron of late autumn bracken, a basket of old-gold russets.

Softened by all the work it's done,
stray hairs from everyone who's come for comfort,
their breath and hers still among its fibres.

After another great meal, she wraps it around me too.
One clack of her bangles, one note of her laugh,
all wolves are gone.

Seasalter

A gusty, slant-lit day. Two dogs
pinball
among low-tide pools. Slate blue.

Rain clouds stoop to the horizon -
ragged warriors
reaching for their swords.

A rusty tinge to the skyline:
another squall
gathers up her skirts.

North Sea rests fists on hips,
eases her back,
leaves foam-sea-spit where it lies.

Rain's naughty children,
all in armour,
run hand in hand across our roofs.

Sunshine hums a patient
lullaby,
knits new gloves of beloved's love.

High Winds

'We must free ourselves of the hope that the sea will ever rest. We must learn to sail in high winds.' Attributed to Aristotle Onassis

Hooligan breakers wallop the shore,
cuff the shingle,
haul it home drenched.

Kohl-eyed gannets swoop and plunge
to bandit rhythms
only they can hear.

Each dropped-crystal wave
shatters
over boulders, spatters dark, blown kisses.

In the crook of the moonlit
harbour arm,
crosswinds settle age-old scores.

Swell slackens its hold,
folds like old sheets,
meek as a perfect drying day.

A swirl of petticoats; the sea
recedes.
Gulls tap-dance in her traces.

A cockle shell caps my finger,
strokes the full of my lip -
a sea kiss.

Glory of a wide sky:
the higher we look,
the more we find our feet.

Away in a Beach Hut

Let loose from indoor turkey-fog,
we stream
along the shore like bubbles.

Curlews revolve high through
south-westerlies,
dissolve into mudflat mists.

Christmas pudding simmers on the
gas ring,
encircled by kissed faces.

Gulls explore shingle for clams.
Children
double-check wrapping for missed gifts.

Deckchairs crunch into their own
beached dignity
under the Milky Way.

Tumble-sleet swirls a single
scalloped
blanket across the oyster beds.

With rich stories and songs,
chipped teacups
of hot rum, we toast the tide's turn.

In the Cool of This Hottest Day

Another day closes its
sunset eye.
At least it watched me writing.

How do I write joy? Peg
phrases
on pages, spun laundry in the sun.

Tonight, I will wear party black,
celebrate
the death of past ordeals.

Turn over any heart. Count
nicks, scars.
Admire the flinty shine. The weight.

We hew more truth with our pieces than
wreckers
ever wreak in breaking.

Blackbird threads notes through this frayed
evening's quilt,
stitches the day together.

In the cool of the close of this
hottest day,
I sense my life begin.

Oyster Seventeens

The sea nestles me; my
best mother.
I flip and twirl like a seal pup.

This skin, dulled under hospital lights,
exults
in blustery sunshine.

Where sea and sky merge in a
thousand pinks
aligns the mind's horizon.

Twilight wraps blankets of
crimson glory
around this evening's shoulders.

Sky is honeyed mango slivers,
dark-rum-soaked,
with pomegranate seeds.

Laughter waltzes with garlic prawns,
jives with olives,
pirouettes with wine.

Between the bowls and candlelight
stretch moments
of perfect contentment.

Seaweed garlands roll on the high
tide, full
moon's tangle of jet and jade.

This fresh day. Let's shuck it
open, feel
gusto pour between our fingers.

Pure Blue

Beside me walks the other life I might have had.
We swim together, she and I, float, dip our heads,
the wide air light around us. Free in every pore.
She so many decades deep in love security,
she wears it like skin.

Buoyed by new-found safety,
I whoop and tumble laughing in the waves
and the spray sings:
'You can lay your armour down now.
You can trust your wounds to heal.'

During the worst, a dream recurred: a man and place I never knew.
In the warmth of an evening garden together we'd let the day's work
drift away. All kind smiling eyes, he'd hand me a glass of wine.

Curlews bank on breezes across pure blue.
I sense the under-thrum of heartbeats one to another,
hear the ancient call to keep building, and the tide's
applause before our efforts wash away.

Happy the Woman

(after Horace's Ode 3.29, trans. John Dryden)

Happy the woman whose sweetest days
stroll with the tide's roll, calmly sway.

Happy the woman whose body's her own -
loosened in moonstone sea foam.

Happy the woman alone with her keys.
Her shoulders ease. Hard won peace.

Happy the woman who sings, jives, sashays
in her own private cabaret.

Happy is she who plants old wounds southward,
delights in all the flowers.

Happy is she in her dinghy 'Astray' -
bound for her love's hideaway.

Happy at one, alone with the moon,
they're easy in their snug cocoon.

Happy the woman who can say,
'I have loved and I have lived today'.

Just the Ticket

(after Dylan Thomas)

Do not go reckless into love, my girl.
Beware of skilful charms at close of day.
Wrapped in romance, watch out for churls.

Wise women before you have hurled
their senses and their plans astray.
Do not go reckless into love, my girl.

Good wives, their patience drained, turned taciturn,
dream of silken beds and wild sea spray
wrapped in far romance, all flags unfurled.

Untamed, we weave our talents in high swirls,
learn too late the price such courage pays:
do not go reckless into love, my girl.

Old women know with private smiles downturned
the female joys and burdens, all the ways
we wrap our secrets safe, count pleasures earned.

And you, young woman, sound advice all spurned,
your heart trussed up in white lace and bouquets…
May all be well in your new hopeful world
but treasure this, my gift: pre-paid return.

Nayland Rock Shelter, 2022

'On Margate Sands … I can connect Nothing with nothing':
T S Eliot, *The Waste Land* (1922)

August is the stickiest month,
seaside
as ever the perfect host.

Blousy old girl, yellowed fingers,
a cough,
Margate embraces us all.

Last night sea fists, dark as spit-flecked
bronco hides,
punched low skies black and blue.

Calm beyond the storm. Ructions stowed
neatly
back on shelves. Storm-washed. Repaired.

Veiled sunshine shakes out her
spangled gown
over miles of silver billows.

We run, crabs loose from a spilt
green bucket,
back to the best of childhood.

Content with plastic spades,
we burrow
where our simplest selves can find us.

On Margate Sands songs and laughter
ride the winds,
connect us all with all.

Laughing and Grief: Paris, 2020

This is the meal I came for: suprême de volaille with dauphinoises followed by chocolate mousse on shortbread with a marinated pear and two swirls of jus. Now cognac.

Through the window's gold lettering, the street is drying in sunlight. It's been a proper Parisian meal, all understated expertise, not a vegetable in sight, and here winding through the exuberant voices comes my café crème.

My coat is still damp on the empty chair across my table, and I toast it as if it's my father. He adored Europe and hauled us all as teenagers to campsites the length and breadth of it. Our Irish island could never contain my dad any more than a conventional marriage could. In my memory's caverns, he's holding my baby brother over his head singing 'Say goodbye now to pastimes and play, lad'. As if he were singing to his own unmarried self, though he loved being a father.

Ah yes, *The Marriage of Figaro*. My father in a frock coat measuring for his bridal bed while parents from our school strolled around him in wigs and brocade singing too. I was forty before I realised my mother sent me to those rehearsals with colouring books - the only child there - to remind him, and everybody else, he was a Belfast teacher with a wife and kids.

In my bag, my phone buzzes. Emails started piling up the minute I settled in the Eurostar, and before I'd made it through the Gare du Nord crowds, there were hundreds. I've ignored them all: these three days are ruthlessly scheduled for me. Me alone.

I feel the warmth of you here now, Dad. Or it might be the cognac. I was away on a literary trail to Montparnasse this morning. To find Beckett. Inside the cemetery gates, with rain coming on and no phone, I did my best to memorise the notice showing who was where, and off I went. In the February light, the cemetery had the look of a monochrome ocean floor designed on graph paper. Sections grew into and over each other in a jumble of beached mausoleums and headstones adrift among lichen and moss.

It should have been easy. I couldn't miss Maupassant's memorial for example, surely. A big, fuck-off thing with white railings and his name on a pediment in capitals but could I find it? *Non.* I pounded around where

Beckett was supposed to be. Nothing obviously him so I trawled down the narrow tracks between the graves, then the same exercise crosswise.

So many families. So much money spent – one particularly fancy vault was dedicated to '*Famille de Bully*' and here was I, ignoring them all for a playwright. Had I strayed into one of his plays? Not so much *Waiting for Godot* as Searching for the Great Man himself. Would he ever appear? Would it make any sense if he did?

You would have known where he was, Dad. I longed to phone you, like that time in Edinburgh. I could feel Mr Hyde scampering up every shadowy side-street but where was Stevenson himself? You answered my call immediately, as always, and told me how Stevenson, his wife and the dog, all of them perpetually unwell, moved to Eastern Samoa for the good of their health. Until, at the age of only forty-four, Stevenson died there of an aneurism pulling the cork from a bottle of exceptional red. It was the exit you'd hoped for yourself.

I was about to go when I heard a voice: '*Vous cherchez quelqu'un*?'

A small man in his eighties stood there, his eyes all gentleness when he smiled, all loneliness when he didn't. He was Henri, he said, lived close by. With droplets shining on his black overcoat, scarf and large sheepskin gloves, he was oblivious to what had turned to sleet, even when drips hung from his nose and earlobes. He guided me the few paces to Beckett's plain granite slab, unmissable on the main path, with a single pot of heather. In exactly the right section.

Had I seen the others, Henri asked. There wasn't another living soul around us. '*Suivez-moi*.'

Sleet draped lace everywhere and together our steps melted Henri's single line of footsteps. He walked with a geriatric shuffle, pointing to a famous grave here or there - Baudelaire, Saint-Saens - until one of the huge gloves slid loose and dropped at his feet. He bent painfully, refusing help, tucked it into his coat and slid both his hands into the other one. He wobbled his thumbs around in their narrow space as if he were making a rabbit shadow on a wall, grinning: '*Plus chaud comme cela*.' I could see exactly what sort of little boy he'd been.

Parisian *amour* for their flawed celebrities clearly survives *la mort*. Memorabilia at Chirac's grave was fruit, toys, baskets of violets left by grandchildren perhaps, or mistresses. Serge Gainsbourg sang about some metro station or other so tourists ask at the station if they can keep their tickets and leave them, each with a pebble on top, for Serge. The joint grave for De Beauvoir and Sartre is glorious pink marble covered in red and coral lipstick kisses. Defiant French kisses.

Gravel crunched behind us; we were no longer alone. A hundred feet away an elegant young Chinese woman in a black face mask and trench coat sauntered along the central promenade, eyes only for her phone. Nothing remarkable there except for four soldiers in square formation around her, also in masks, their rifles cocked and ready. At the gates, they swung left onto the street.

She mesmerised me. Her structured solitude, as if she carried a fortress around her more visibly than I did. Was she from Wuhan, was this her isolation? I didn't have a face mask. Should I get one?

A nudge at my elbow was Henri guiding me again. There was agitation in his shuffle as we approached a plain grave near the exit.

Pebbles traced out a heart shape and in the middle under a white stone was a laminated Valentine's card. Jean Seberg, 1938 – 1979. Henri stood and bent his bare head. His hands, still together in their single glove, met under his chin as if in prayer.

I had no idea who she was or how this beautiful American with a stack of Hollywood films to her credit had such impact here in Paris. Henri explained, tears lighting his eyes: her marriages, her so-called suicide, the FBI's apology for hounding her, her search for safe ground, her tragedy.

'We are nothing more than dust and shadow,' he muttered in French.

'Horace', I said. My father taught Classics - Laughing and Grief, as the Mock Turtle used to say - and read, talked, joked so much in Latin, my mother forbade it anywhere near her. He yielded eventually, saying he would be thankful not to be *persona non grata* in his own home.

Henri beamed, folded away his single glove and lifted my hand in its fitted black leather into his own. How he had enjoyed spending time with someone '*jeune et jolie*', he said, and slowly pressed his lips to my gloved knuckles. We had spoken in nothing but French so far, he politely accepting my efforts, correcting nothing. Now he spoke in English, Dryden's English:

'Happy the man, and happy he alone,

He who can call today his own:

He who, secure within, can say –

Tomorrow, do thy worst, for I have lived today.'

Dear Henri. His flawless courtesy forbade him to acknowledge or even notice how his words breached the crackling force of my seclusion, and the emotional collapse I did my best to hide. Within a handful of seconds, I was immersed in hospital again with you in ICU after that catastrophic operation. The silent nurse at her station, the array of tubes and contraptions, that racking cough that turned you Dickensian puce until you reached for me, my hand, and gripped it until the worst subsided. I creamed your arthritic hands and feet when they flaked, brought you recordings of Figaro and Susanna, read to you – read to you time and again your favourite poet. From your favourite Ode – 3, 29: *Happy the Man.*

In those few seconds at Seberg's grave, I am kissing your forehead again on that last night of your breathing, as everything you knew ebbed away. I am at your graveside in heartless winds during what was always going to be a complicated funeral; so many good-looking senior women who knew you so well, each taking a quiet moment to confide with me, '*Carpe diem*'. Orphaned, stranded, I marvelled at your talent for welcoming love.

My mother hated that talent of course. 'There are worse things than being single,' she used to say, trying to understand my office life. But she was not the parent who loved me. That was you, my father, who first held me while she was stitched and tended, while she nursed her own resentment of me for being female.

You, Dad, flawed husband you may have been, but your promise to love me resounded again and again in the deepest whorls of my ears, a promise made to my child hand resting in yours, to my child eyes and ears experiencing an orchestra for the first time, to my heart when you gave me my first copy of Heaney.

Remember that day you were driving us all the length of France and saw peaches for sale at the roadside? 'Let's get peaches,' you shouted, 'let's get a whole tray!'

Henri allowed my hand to belong to me again and bent for the card on Seberg's grave to show me. *Jamais de désespoir*, it said inside, in elderly French script. 'From you?' I asked. More a blink than a nod told me, yes.

I have thought of Henri often over the past year. He was the last man to kiss me before we lurched into this world of lockdowns, solitude, panic, one crisis after another, lost opportunities, grief.

What are the odds he's still breathing? Whose was the last face he saw before they closed the ambulance door and that world of masked smiles and vinyl kindness absorbed him? Who held his hand? Who read him Horace, whispered '*nil desperandum*'?

We shook hands like the strangers we were, and it wasn't until I was out and beyond the crossing that I was awash with tears. Any restaurant would do, I had to eat and, eyes wiped, I pushed into one with red window frames and gold lettering.

After that meal, with cognac and café crème beside me, I opened my wire-topped journal and began to scribble my way into some sense in all this. When my fingers were exhausted, I leant back and rested my eyes on the sun setting golden at the end of the street.

'It's time, darling.'

Your voice, for me alone.

'It's time to let go now, and live.'

A breath came out of me, something like joy. I paid for my meal and walked out into the evening's glitter back towards the Seine. There was a new swing in my walk, unfamiliar strength. Whatever came my way back home, I was going to welcome it.

Like father, like daughter, I would live my life to the full and embrace love.

It's not been as easy as that, of course. I work from home now, part-time, and help at the food bank. My hair is looser, my heels flatter and though I have less money in the bank, I'm richer than I've ever been.

I'm saving to go back to Montparnasse cemetery where I will sit down by Jean Seberg's grave with a bottle of exceptional red and read Horace until

Henri comes. If Henri does not come, I will leave a message for Jean Seberg anchored by a white stone.

Jamais de désespoir.

Never lose hope.

Acknowledgements with Thanks

OneWorld, *Places of Poetry* anthology, 2020: *Carnlough Bay.*
The Phare*: Cleopatra on Portstewart Strand, Just the Ticket.*
Live Canon: *My Boyish Love, Away in a Beach Hut.*
Mary Evans Picture Library Poems and Pictures blog: *High Winds, Off the Map, Reflection, Oyster Seventeens.*
London Grip*: Palm Tree Victory.*
A New Ulster: *In the Cool of this Hottest Day, On a Scale of One to Ten.*
Arlen House, *Her Other Language*, 2020: Extracts from *Six-Count Jive.*
Fevers of the Mind 'Overcome' anthology, 2021: *Bloodstains on the Stones.*
American Writers Review, 2021: *Laughing and Grief.*

Many thanks also to Leslie Bell of Mica Press, Charlotte Ansell for her wise critique, Graham Taylor for sub-editing, and Henri, the gentleman I met in Montmartre cemetery in February 2020 who so kindly helped me find Beckett's and Seberg's graves. 'Laughing and Grief' amplifies our encounter into fiction. rosiejohnstonwrites.com

So many words. Sung, scribbled,
told by the fire,
by the cradle. Vanished.

In dreams, I hear whispers, women
long gone:
'Find our lost poems. Write them.'

www.ingramcontent.com/pod-product-compliance
Ingram Content Group UK Ltd.
Pitfield, Milton Keynes, MK11 3LW, UK
UKHW050440270225
455623UK00011B/193